Under His Wings

Fear

Discovering That God Is with Us in Fearful Times

(A Study of Psalm 56)

Written by Susan M. Schulz
Edited by Martha Streufert Jander

CPH

Concordia Publishing House

Editorial Assistant: Laura Christian

Copyright © 1999 by Concordia Publishing House
3558 South Jefferson Avenue, St. Louis, MO 63118-3968
Manufactured in the United States of America

This publication is also available in braille and in large print for the visually
impaired. Write to Library for the Blind, 1333 S. Kirkwood Rd., St. Louis,
MO 63122-7295; or call 1-800-433-3954.

Contents

David's Fear

Where Are We Going?

We will take an introductory look at fear—both David's and ours. We will explore fear responses and grow to appreciate more fully our great God's presence and help during fearful times.

Ready, Set, Go

Begin with prayer. Ask God to renew your spirit through the study of His Word and to lead you to a deeper trust in Him.

Spend a few minutes on "**Where Am I Now?**" thinking about the fears we all experience in this life. Get into "**The Search**," remembering that David's God is your God, and that He is the answer for your fears too.

"**Respond**" to God's reassuring Scripture promises with praise and prayer.

Before the next session, do the "**Do**," recording your thoughts and experiences on the journal page and filling in the prayer page (or using it as a way to pray each day).

Where Am I Now?

Take a few minutes to make two lists—children's fears and adults' fears:

What fears or underlying needs are similar for both children and adults? Discuss how our fears change as we grow older.

The Search
In the Grip of Fear

1a. David was afraid. He had been anointed to be the next king of Israel, killed the giant Goliath, and left his fields and flocks to play music in King Saul's court, but he was afraid—with good reason. Saul craved and pursued David's death with the fury of an enemy driven by very powerful fear. Read 1 Samuel 18:6–15, 28–29 to see what Saul's fear drove him to do. Where did Saul's fear come from? How did it lead him into sin?

1b. How do fearful situations lead people into sin today? What desperate responses to fear are evident in today's society? What can the consequences be?

2a. The consequences of Saul's sin against David trapped David himself in a web of deceit and fear. To escape Saul's fear-driven intent to murder, David panicked. Without seeking God's directive, he ran in fear for refuge to the enemy Philistine city of Gath (the birthplace of Goliath, no less). Read 1 Samuel 21:10–15. Why might David have thought Gath a safe haven and King Achish an accommodating benefactor? What had he not counted on? What choices did David make? Why did he react the way he did?

2b. Discuss the fears that have gripped you in the past or at times grip you now. How do you react to these fears? What path of desperation or plan of avoidance tempts you most? How does your response reflect your trust in or lack of faith in God?

3. Like every other sin, a fear response that ignores God and moves ahead in full-speed desperation leads to bigger problems and aching losses. What price did David pay for his desperate response to fear?

In the Hands of God

4. Though David gave into his fear and desperation, God did not abandon him. God was working all along to teach and strengthen him. David appeared to have lost everything—his home, his dignity, his safety; but through it all, God strengthened his faith. Read Psalm 56, the psalm David penned on this occasion, and write below a short summary of David's rediscovered help in times of fear.

5a. As a sinner, David would never *perfectly* trust and look to God in times of fear. What verses in the psalm indicate David's struggle to keep focused on his God? Underline the verses where David voices his fear. Place a check mark or underline with a different color pen the verses where David expresses his trust in God.

5b. Which verses are meaningful to you? How might they help as you struggle to keep focused on God?

6a. As God provided David, He still provides us with a very important tool in keeping our focus on Him even in times of fear. Read Psalm 56:4, 10. How is God's Word an important tool? How did David use it? How might you use it or help someone else to use it?

David had God's Word in several forms. He had the writings of Moses and the promises spoken to him through the prophet Samuel. God's Word reassured David of His forgiving love. God's Word changed David's fear to faith. God's Word has the power to change our fears to faith as well.

6b. Which promises of God recorded in Scripture can you remember when you face fearful times? Use one of these in your closing prayer.

Respond

Whether our fear is the result of our own sin or the sins of others against us, we have God's promise to deliver us from stumbling—even to the point of death. God rescues us from our present fears and He rescued us especially from the greatest fear of all—eternal death—by the death and resurrection of His own Son. Now we may indeed "walk before God in the light of life" (Psalm 56:13).

As a group, respond to God's words of reassurance with joyful praise by reading aloud Psalm 56:10–13 from the same translation. Have the leader read the first half of each verse and the participants respond with the second half. Start out softly and gradually increase in volume.

In your closing prayer, thank God for one of the promises you listed in question 6b. Also pray for the Holy Spirit's power to look to God and wait for His deliverance and peace in times of fear.

Do

Write in your journal this week about your fears and how they influence your behavior (refer to question 2b). Jot down a verse of reassurance from Psalm 56 after each listed fear.

Additional Bible readings for this week: Acts 16:22–34; Romans 8:28–39; and 2 Corinthians 1:3–11. Copy and attach to a mirror or other place you see daily, the words of 2 Corinthians 1:10 or Romans 8:32 to remind you of God's constant care and protection.

Use the prayer starters each day as you come to the Lord in your quiet time, either writing in your own endings to the sentences or leaving them blank to be used in a new way each day.

For next week, read through and think about Session 2, filling in any responses as you like.

Journal Page

O Lord, You are so _____

_____

_____

_____

and I am so _____

_____

_____

_____

Please forgive me for _____

_____

_____

_____

Help me _____

_____

_____

_____

Please bless and take care of _____

_____

_____

_____

Thanks, Lord, for _____

_____

_____

_____

God Keeps Hagar Safe

Where Are We Going?

We will study God's care of Hagar in her times of fear and realize that Hagar's God is the same God who responds to our fearful situations with loving care for us as well.

Ready, Set, Go

Begin with prayer. Ask God to fill you with His Spirit as you study His Word so your heart is made sure in His love and mercy.

Spend a few minutes on **"Where Am I Now?"** thinking about your needs in times of fear and how you attempt to meet those needs. As you do **"The Search,"** notice God's faithfulness in Hagar's times of need and realize His faithfulness in your times of need.

"Respond" to our unchanging God by expressing a deep trust in Him through the words of Psalm 56.

Before the next session, do the **"Do."** Express your thoughts and experiences on the journal page and use the prayer starters to help you in your prayer life.

Where Am I Now?

Discuss something that you ran from as a child and/or as a teenager. What made you afraid? To what did you run?

The Search

Hagar in the Grip of Fear

Abram and Sarai were childless, yet God had

promised that Abram's seed would be as numerous as the stars in the sky (Genesis 15:5). Sarai became discouraged with waiting, and in Genesis 16:1–6 we read how she takes it into her own hands to provide an heir for her husband. Sarai gives Hagar, her Egyptian maidservant, to Abram so that he can father a child by her. Hagar does indeed become pregnant and flaunts it in front of her childless mistress. When Sarai harshly reprimands her, Hagar is rebellious and afraid and flees into the desert, likely to go back to Egypt.

1a. What do you think Hagar was running from? What were the fears she faced? What might she have hoped to find by returning to Egypt?

1b. What makes you run from situations? What makes you afraid in those situations? What have you run from recently? What provides you with comfort, courage, and security when you are afraid?

2a. Read Genesis 16:7–16. What words of discipline did the angel of the LORD speak to Hagar? Why do you think God waited until Hagar was in the wilderness before confronting her? Why do you suppose the angel called her the "servant of Sarai"?

2b. Why does the Lord not seem to rescue us immediately from our perils and fears? What lessons might He want to teach us?

3a. What words of comfort did the angel tell Hagar? Why do you suppose He sent her back into the fearful situation with Sarai? Why could Hagar respond the way she did?

3b. How has God helped you walk back into fearful situations? Why can you respond with obedience and joy? What words of comfort does God give you?

Our God Who Sees and Responds

4a. Read Psalm 56 and discuss what theme both David, in Psalm 56:8, and Hagar, in Genesis 16:13, express. Write the theme below.

4b. This theme is evident in Hagar's life once again in Genesis 21:8–20. As you read the account, notice God's response to Hagar and Ishmael's fearful situation. How does this account beautifully illustrate the truth of Psalm 56:8 and Genesis 16:13?

5a. It is comforting to know that God sees us and records our tears, but the real comfort goes one step further. How did Hagar know God had seen her? Why is this important for us to know?

5b. Share a time in your own life or in the life of someone you know when God's actions beautifully illustrated God's notice of tears. How did the situation (or you) change as a result?

6. Sometimes, however, we cannot see or understand God's response to our tears. Satan tempts us during these times to turn away from God. We can so easily fall into the sin of mistrust. What can we hold on to in order to make it through these times?

God's Word in Times of Fear

When David was in danger and full of fear, the Holy Spirit brought to his mind words of Scripture. These words of the Lord brought great comfort and strength to David, as evidenced by his words of praise in Psalm 56.

7a. How might Hagar have used verses 4 and 10–11 of Psalm 56 as words of praise?

7b. How does God speak to us today? What means has He provided to strengthen us in times of fear?

15

Respond

Hebrews 13:8 says, "Jesus Christ is the same yesterday and today and forever." The Jesus who may have come to Hagar in the form of the angel of the LORD and the Jesus who came to earth to die for us has not changed. In His love, He still comes to us today and responds to our fears. We have direct access to His power and grace through the Word and Sacraments. We can fight the sin of mistrust with God-given strength. Through His power, we can rise above our fears to a hope and joy only the Lord can give.

Read Psalm 56:13 in pairs. Substitute your partner's name appropriately. Then read the verse together with the whole group.

As you bring your prayers to the Lord today, include any concerns shared earlier and especially those facing fearful situations. After each prayer request, respond with the entire group, "In God [we] trust; [we] will not be afraid" (Psalm 56:4).

Do

In your journal this week, write about fearful times in your life and how the sin of mistrust may have tempted you. Also note how God noticed your struggle and what actions He took on your behalf. Write about other Bible characters who received God's care and rescue in times of fear. Then record in your journal the words of Hebrews 13:8 to remind yourself that God has not changed. He is still active in our times of fear.

Read additional evidence of God's loving care in times of fear: Genesis 28:10–22; Matthew 8:23–27; and John 20:10–20. Copy and attach to your refrigerator or other place you see daily the words of Hebrews 13:8 or John 16:33.

For next week, read the entire book of Esther in the Bible and read through Session 3, writing responses in the spaces provided.

Journal Page

_____
_____
_____
_____
_____
_____
_____
_____
_____
_____
_____
_____
_____
_____
_____
_____
_____
_____
_____
_____
_____
_____
_____
_____
_____
_____
_____
_____
_____

O Lord, You are so _____

_____

_____

_____

and I am so _____

_____

_____

_____

Please forgive me for _____

_____

_____

_____

Help me _____

_____

_____

_____

Please bless and take care of _____

_____

_____

_____

Thanks, Lord, for _____

_____

_____

_____

God Works through Esther

Where Are We Going?

As we study God's directing of Esther's life, we will grow in trust that our powerful, loving God has a wonderful plan for our lives as well.

Ready, Set, Go

Begin with prayer. Ask God to be with you as you study His Word, to strengthen your faith in His leading and guidance, and to help you trust in His plans for you.

Spend a few minutes on "**Where Am I Now?**" Discover your beliefs about God's control of our lives and how these beliefs affect your fears. As you do "**The Search,**" notice God's actions in the life of Esther so you can grow in trust of God's actions in your own life.

"**Respond**" to God with repentance and renewed trust as you close with prayer.

Before the next session, do the "**Do,**" recording your thoughts and experiences on the journal page. Fill in the prayer page or use it as a way to pray each day.

Where Am I Now?

Mark the following true or false; discuss your answers.

____ God controls the results of world elections.

____ Every ruler or world power exists only by God's permission.

____ Events in my life are determined mostly by chance and circumstance.

____ God *works through* all that happens to me, but does not directly *control* what happens to me.

19

How would differing beliefs about the preceding statements influence your fears?

The Search

Esther in the Grip of God

Though God is never directly mentioned in the Book of Esther, He is directly involved in all that happens. This book records no miraculous plagues or parting of seas, but God rescues His people just the same. God's actions in Esther are much like His actions today. He quietly uses people—placing them where they are needed, and directing seemingly coincidental circumstances to accomplish His plan of rescue and salvation.

1. Esther may have been even unaware of God working in her day-to-day life. In general, how aware are we of God working in our day-to-day lives?

2. To realize God's grip on Esther's life and on the lives of those around her, read the following Scripture excerpts. After each section, write a brief summary and discuss this question: How did God direct, control, and use the events recorded here?

a. Esther 2:2–17

b. Esther 2:21–23

When has God arranged for you to be in the right place at the right time?

    c. Esther 3:1–11

    d. Esther 4:1–16

    e. Esther 5:1–3; 7:3–7

    f. Esther 6:1–2

Share a time when God used seemingly small coincidences in your life or in the life or a friend to bring about something important for you and/or for the good of His kingdom.

    g. Esther 8:2–9:3

3a. Look back over your summaries of the verses. When did God's plan of rescue actually begin?

3b. How does realizing that God sets His plan into motion long before crises even start, comfort and strengthen you in your own times of crises?

4a. God's plan could have been road-blocked by fear (Esther 4:11). Where did Esther's strength and courage come from? How had she been encouraged by her uncle Mordecai?

4b. Sometimes we, too, do amazing things even in the midst of our fears. When have your courageous acts amazed you? How were you encouraged by God's Word or by other Christians? In what ways could you see God at work in those times?

5. How can a renewed trust in God's timing, control, and directing of your life affect your fears?

6. Read Psalm 56. Which verses particularly apply to Esther and God's people in this account?

Respond

We have seen how God used His power and control over the events in Esther's life to work good for her and for His people. We know how God used His power through the life, death, and resurrection of Jesus Christ to assure our salvation and the promise of heaven. Is it surprising, then, that God uses His power for our good, to guide and direct our life—even seemingly insignificant events through which He makes His love to us known and accomplishes good for His kingdom? Esther's God is our God. He is working His good and gracious plan in our lives.

With one or two partners, share what you believe God's plans are for you for the next week.

Then praise God together for working through you to accomplish His will for Him and His kingdom. Bring to His gracious hand any concerns that have arisen during the study.

Do

This week keep your eyes open for little "coincidences" that help you see God at work in your life or give you opportunities to share His love with others in word and deed. In your journal, write about these times or other times you remember, expressing your deepening trust in God's hand at work in your life.

For further evidence of God's direction in the lives of His people, read the story of Joseph in Genesis 37:12–36; 39; 41:1–43; and particularly 45:4–11.

For next week, read through Session 4 and fill in responses as you wish.

Journal Page

O Lord, You are so _____
_____
_____

and I am so _____
_____
_____
_____

Please forgive me for _____
_____
_____
_____

Help me _____
_____
_____
_____
_____

Please bless and take care of _____
_____
_____
_____
_____

Thanks, Lord, for _____
_____
_____
_____
_____

Session 4

Our God: All Faithful, All Powerful

Where Are We Going?

Today as we explore the contrasts in Psalm 56, we will realize the powerlessness of our enemies and rejoice in our faithful, all-powerful God.

Ready, Set, Go

Begin with prayer. Ask God to open your eyes and heart to His presence in your times of fear and to break down the walls that keep you from seeing His love.

Spend a few minutes on **"Where Am I Now?"** drawing or describing an enemy that threatens your present security. Use **"The Search"** to loosen the enemy's hold on you and to open your eyes to the power and faithfulness of God.

Use the words of Psalm 56 to **"Respond"** to God with renewed confidence and trust and leave your fears with Him in prayer.

Finally, do the **"Do,"** recording your thoughts and experiences on the journal page. Fill in the prayer page or use it as a way to pray each day.

Where Am I Now?

In the following space, draw a picture of an enemy. Next to the enemy, draw a picture of yourself. Before you start, consider who or what the enemy is in your life right now; how big the enemy seems compared to you, and what kind of hold the enemy has on you (e.g.,

26

around the neck, merely grasping a toe, etc.). You may label the enemy if you wish. If you are uncomfortable drawing, write a description of the picture instead.

The Search

At times an enemy's grip on our lives and the fear that comes with it are so tight and suffocating that we can do nothing but struggle for breath and cry in agony. Today as we study three major comparisons highlighted in Psalm 56, the enemy's grip of fear will be loosened and our trust in God will grow.

The Power of the Enemy Versus the Power of God

1a. Read Psalm 56:1–6 and jot down the characteristics of the enemy.

1b. How is the enemy described in verse 4? What does this important characteristic tell you about the power of the enemy?

2a. Now make a note of the evidences of God's power as recorded in verses 7–9.

2b. The verses we have studied so far help us realize that David's enemies were mere mortals puffed up with pride but with no *real* power. Real power rests with God alone. When you are afraid of an enemy who can harm the body but cannot kill the soul (Matthew 10:28), how can this knowledge of God's power comfort and strengthen you?

The Words of the Enemy Versus the Words of God

3a. Record and discuss a description of the truth and validity of the words spoken by enemies (Psalm 56:2, 5). Then record and discuss a description of the truth and validity of God's words.

3b. As you look at the two lists, discuss why we sinful human beings are so prone to believing the words of the enemy and discounting the promises of God.

4a. How does knowing that God never lies (Titus 1:2) and that He has all power to back up His Word strengthen you in times of fear?

4b. Add a drawing of God's powerful hand surrounding your "Where Am I Now?" picture.

4c. God's words and His power to back them up brought praise to David's heart. Read Psalm 56:4, 10–11. Discuss how these same words of praise could be used appropriately in your life today.

Death Versus Life

5. Read Psalm 56:11–13, remembering that David's situation had not yet changed; he was merely expressing his sure and certain hope. What was the basis of this hope? How is hope in total opposition to death?

6a. The concept of *death* in the psalms encompasses all that diminishes life. Sickness, anxiety, weakness, evil threats, and conflicts are all experiences with death. What aspects of death are diminishing your life right now?

6b. How does walking "in the light of life"—going through life hand in hand with God—help you rise above these experiences and deliver you from every form of death's power?

7. What a difference God makes in this earthly life of struggle and death! Describe the joy and peace that are ours even in fearful times as we walk in our God-given "light of life."

Respond

As we are reminded of God's power, His words of truth, and His triumph over death, our confidence soars. By now your picture of the enemy needs some changes. Perhaps your enemy seems smaller and can no longer retain his stranglehold on you. Perhaps the only change is God's powerful hand surrounding you. Choose a verse of the psalm that expresses your renewed trust in your God and share the verse and the reason you chose it with a partner or the entire group.

Bring your fears, problems, and praises before the Lord through prayer, then close by reading the following together: "I will present my thank offerings to You. For You have delivered me from death and my feet from stumbling, that I may walk before God in the light of life" (Psalm 56:12–13).

Do

Begin your journal writing this week by writing down the words of Romans 8:31b. Express in your journal how this verse and Psalm 56 can help you through a current struggle with an enemy or the power of death as defined in question 6a.

Additional readings this week: Psalm 34; Psalm 91; and 1 John 4:4–18. Place the words of Romans 8:31b where you will see them frequently.

Continue with regular Bible reading, prayer, journaling, and worship in your walk with God as He continues to fill you with renewed trust and faith.

Journal Page

O Lord, You are so _____

_____

_____

_____

and I am so _____

_____

_____

_____

Please forgive me for _____

_____

_____

_____

_____

Help me _____

_____

_____

_____

_____

Please bless and take care of _____

_____

_____

_____

_____

Thanks, Lord, for _____

_____

_____

_____

_____

O Lord, You are so

and I am so

Please forgive me for

Help me

Please bless and take care of

Thanks, Lord, for

Confidence

Seeing God's Presence in Our Times
of Confidence

(A Study of Psalm 91)

Written by Susan M. Schulz
Edited by Martha Streufert Jander

Concordia Publishing House

Editorial Assistant: Laura Christian

This publication is also available in braille and in large print for the visually
impaired. Write to Library for the Blind, 1333 S. Kirkwood Rd., St. Louis,
MO 63122-7295; or call 1-800-433-3954.

Contents

Moses, Man of God

Where Are We Going?

In today's lesson, we will look back at God's powerful deliverance of His people from Egypt in order to
help us grow in confidence of God's power and presence
as we look ahead to our own future.

Ready, Set, Go

Begin with prayer. Ask for the Holy Spirit's wisdom
and power to see God's work in the past and grow in
confidence of God's hand in the present and future.

Spend a few minutes on "**Where Am I Now?**" rating
your levels of confidence and thinking about sources of
confidence. Get into "**The Search.**" As you study Moses
and Psalm 91, let God's Word strengthen your sense of
security in the hands of God.

"**Respond**" to your look back at Scripture by looking back at God's help in your own life and using song
to express your renewed confidence in Him.

Before the next session, do the "**Do.**" Record your
faith journey on the journal page and use the prayer
page as you like.

Where Am I Now?

Rate your level of confidence in yourself from 0 (least
amount) to 10 (most) in each of the following situations:
_____ Starting a new job
_____ Using a new recipe when you have dinner guests
_____ Making financial decisions
_____ Choosing new clothes
_____ Speaking, reading, or performing in front of a group

Has your level of confidence in any of these areas grown over the years? If yes, what prompted the growth?

The Search

Remember Moses, God's great prophet and leader of one of God's most spectacular acts of deliverance? Surely Moses was a man of infinite confidence—or was he? As we read portions of the life of Moses and his conversations with God, perhaps we will see a person more like ourselves—capable of great confidence, but at times full of fear and doubt.

Moses' Doubts and Fears

1. Moses was a Hebrew adopted by Pharaoh's daughter and raised as a prince of Egypt. When he was grown, he saw an Egyptian beating a Hebrew. Moses killed the Egyptian. Read what happened afterwards in Exodus 2:14–15 and rate Moses' level of confidence from 0 (least) to 10 (most) in each of the following:
Himself _____ God _____ His own safety _____

2a. God had much work to do in, with, and for Moses. Read Exodus 3:3–11 and record Moses' response to God's call.

2b. God was not put off by Moses' doubts and fears. Read Exodus 3:12–14 and 4:1–17, then discuss God's responses to Moses. List each doubt or fear and the corresponding response from God.

God Responds

3a. As you look at the preceding list, how would you describe God's handling of Moses' doubts, fears, and unwillingness? What did God want Moses to know about Him?

3b. What reassurance does this provide when you are afraid and full of doubt? What does God want you to know about Him? How does He accomplish this?

Songs of Confidence

4a. The rest of Moses' story reveals how his confidence grew with every act of God on behalf of His people and came to a peak after the parting of the Red Sea. Read Moses' song of confidence in Exodus 15:1–18. Jot down a few phrases that seem to express best Moses' confidence. Why could Moses not have composed this song in his early days? How and why did his confidence grow?

4b. Share, as you feel comfortable, a time in your life when your confidence in God soared. How can you take advantage of the memory of what God did for you at that time?

5a. Let's consider another Scripture song of confidence, Psalm 91. We are not told who wrote this psalm, but the thoughts it expresses certainly could reflect the content of Moses' heart after God's deliverance from Egypt. As you read the psalm, note and discuss any verses fulfilled literally for God's people during the times of the plagues and the deliverance from Egypt.

5b. What verses of Psalm 91 have been fulfilled literally in your life? Share a time when you rested "in the shadow of the Almighty" (v. 1); felt His angels guarding you (v. 11); and/or called to God and knew His answer (v. 15). Discuss especially how God has shown you His salvation (v. 16).

Respond

Moses' confidence in God grew as he again and again saw and experienced God's power and love for His people. Our confidence in God grows as we look ahead with the same eyes of faith that have looked back and seen God's actions on our behalf.

Sometimes our eyes of faith are blinded by sin, and we have trouble seeing God's work in our lives. In those times, it is especially important to turn to Bible history. The deliverance of God's people from Egypt preserved the line from which the Savior would come—which is part of *our* history. God did it not only for the people of Israel, but also for us so that Jesus would be born and die on the cross for *our* sins. If your confidence in God is weak from your troubles, look back on the history of

your salvation in the words of Scripture. Look back with eyes of faith to see God's presence and power in your life. Confidently sing or read together the hymn "Our God, Our Help in Ages Past":

> Our God, our help in ages past,
>> Our hope for years to come,
> Our shelter from the stormy blast,
>> And our eternal home.

Close with prayer. Include any prayer concerns expressed during the lesson today and end by reading together Psalm 91:2.

Do

In your journal this week, compose a song of confidence. Praise God in your song for His deliverance from specific trials you remember from years gone by. Praise Him for showing you the way of salvation. Express your trust in His continued care and love.

For further faith growth this week, read the following portions of Scripture, keeping in mind that these historical accounts are part of *your* salvation history: Psalm 20; 1 Samuel 17; John 19:1–20:9. Write the words of Psalm 20:7b on a sticky note and place it where you will see it often.

For next week, read through Lesson 2 and fill in any responses as you wish.

Journal Page

O Lord, You are so _____

_____

_____

_____

and I am so _____

_____

_____

_____

Please forgive me for _____

_____

_____

_____

Help me _____

_____

_____

_____

Please bless and take care of _____

_____

_____

_____

_____

Thanks, Lord, for _____

_____

_____

_____

_____

Session 2
Mary, Woman of Confidence

Where Are We Going?

In today's lesson, we will study a New Testament woman of confidence, Jesus' mother, Mary. We will investigate the role of pondering and then submitting to God's will in her life and in the life of any confident Christian.

Ready, Set, Go

Begin with prayer. Pray that the Lord will bless your study of His Word; ask for a measure of the Holy Spirit's wisdom and power so you can more easily submit your future to His care.

Spend a few minutes on **"Where Am I Now?"** to consider your pondering and submission tendencies. Then move on to **"The Search"** to learn more about living a confident life with the Lord.

In the **"Respond"** section, express your confidence in God by reading Mary's song from Luke 1; close with prayer and praise.

Before the next session, do the **"Do."** Record your thoughts on the journal page and use the prayer page as you like.

Where Am I Now?

Put the corresponding number on the lines below to indicate how you spend your "pondering" time. Discuss your answers as you feel comfortable. Time I spend
Little _____ Much _____

    1. Pondering things going wrong in my life.

    2. Pondering the many good things God has done for me.

3. Fighting God's plan for my life.

4. Calmly and confidently submitting to God's plans for my life.

The Search
A Woman of Confidence

1a. In the Bible, Jesus' mother, Mary, is portrayed as a woman of confidence. Let's search the Scriptures to understand better Mary's confident, calm way of handling a very eventful life. We are first introduced to Mary when the angel Gabriel tells her that she is to be the mother of the long-promised Savior. Read Mary's response in Luke 1:34–38. Then write a short description of her response and attitude toward God.

1b. Mary very clearly portrayed a willingness to submit to God's plan for her life. What does this indicate about her confidence in God? Why was her confidence in God and not in herself? What did submission to God do for Mary?

1c. Refer to "Where Am I Now?" How did you rate on your submission to God's plans for you? What can submission do for you? What happens when we fight to do our own thing, go our own way? What does our sinful tendency to fight submission to God's plan for our life show? What is God's solution for us?

Pondering Builds Confidence

Now read Luke 2:15–19, 41–51 and John 2:1–5. Twice in these accounts, we read that Mary treasured and pondered in her heart the amazing and sometimes confusing events of her life as the mother of Jesus.

2a. What events did Mary ponder? How did her ponderings influence her confidence in God and her calm acceptance of His will? How did her ponderings affect her absolute confidence that Jesus could and would help at the wedding at Cana?

2b. We may think that pondering has to take place in our heads, but Mary pondered in her heart. What is the difference? How does pondering in our faith-filled hearts change our interpretation of events in our lives?

2c. What treasures of God have you pondered lately? What might you plan to ponder during the next week? How will this help your confidence in the Lord and your acceptance of His will grow?

Psalm 91

3a. Perhaps one of Mary's favorite psalms was Psalm 91. Read the first two verses of the psalm. How do these verses so aptly portray Mary's attitude and life?

3b. How can we get this kind of an attitude? How could this kind of attitude benefit us in our lives?

4. Read Psalm 91:14. Why would Jesus' death and resurrection fulfill this verse for Mary? for us? How did Jesus provide protection for Mary even as He hung on the cross (John 19:26–27)?

5a. This psalm may have been Mary's song of confidence. What other verses might Mary have taken joy in at the time of Jesus' death? Why? At His resurrection?

5b. What verses of Psalm 91 might you ponder on in the future? What do those verses say to you about God's love for you and His plan for your life? What has He already done for you and through you for His kingdom?

Respond

The study of Mary's confidence would not be complete without her song. Use the song to express your own growing confidence in God. In pairs, read Luke 1:46b–49, substituting your partner's name for *me* and *my*. Then, as a group, read verses 50–55 responsively, with

the leader reading the first half of each verse and the participants reading the second half. After the reading, recall and speak any mighty acts God has done for you.

Close with prayer. First bring your petitions before the Lord, then take turns one by one praising and thanking God for one of His mighty or merciful acts on your behalf.

Do

Use your journal this week to help you ponder God's daily actions on your behalf. Write how God's strength and power bring you through each day's troubles and trials and how He gives you joy in the midst of them (or how He has done so in the past).

Ponder on the following passages in the coming week: Psalm 111; 2 Corinthians 1:3–7. Write Luke 1:49 on a sticky note and put it up on your mirror or refrigerator to ponder each time you see it.

For next week, read through Lesson 3 and fill in any blanks as you choose.

Journal Page

O Lord, You are so _____

_____

_____

_____

and I am so _____

_____

_____

_____

Please forgive me for _____

_____

_____

_____

_____

Help me _____

_____

_____

_____

_____

Please bless and take care of _____

_____

_____

_____

_____

Thanks, Lord, for _____

_____

_____

_____

_____

Session 3

Shunammite Woman of Faith

Where Are We Going?

In today's lesson, we will consider the wings of faith that God gave to a Shunammite woman (and also gives to us) and how confidence in the Lord helps us through difficult and even tragic times.

Ready, Set, Go

Begin with prayer. Ask God to make your wings of faith strong to fly above the arrows and plagues and pestilences of this life.

Spend a few minutes on **"Where Am I Now?"** considering different ways to handle a difficult situation. Then move on to **"The Search"** to learn more about the benefits of confidently seeking God and His purpose in times of trouble.

In the **"Respond"** section, consider again your wings of faith and stretch them wide with the confidence only God can bring.

Before the next session, do the **"Do,"** recording your thoughts and experiences on the journal page and filling in the prayer page (or using it as a way to pray each day).

Where Am I Now?

Pretend you are standing at the edge of a busy highway. You desperately need to get to the other side. What would you do?

Now pretend you are a duck. Would you waddle across as fast as your little webbed feet could carry you? Or would you fly?

The Search
Her Wings of Faith

1. Let's take a look at the wings of faith of a woman from Shunem. Read 2 Kings 4:8–14 and, in the space below, write a description of the woman from Shunem and her life situation. Also describe her faith. What does the fact that she did not want to accept any payment from Elisha say about her?

2a. Even though the Shunammite woman was well-to-do, the fact that she had no son and her husband was old meant she might spend many years as a widow with no one to care for her. Read 2 Kings 4:15–17 to see how God provided for this woman of faith. Why do you think she at first objected to Elisha's promise of a son?

2b. How has God surprised you lately with His care and blessings? How did you react? What boost did it give your faith?

Clipped Wings

3a. No doubt the Shunammite woman praised God for the gift of a son. No doubt she took great pride and joy in her boy and the God who had given him to her.

The same God who had blessed her, however, also allowed tragedy to enter her life. Read 2 Kings 4:18–20. Imagine the feelings of this mother. Why do you believe God would allow such a thing to happen?

3b. Now read 2 Kings 4:21–30 and describe in the space below, the woman's confident response.

4a. The Shunammite woman had definitely experienced "the plague that destroys at midday" (Psalm 91:6). Her son lay dead, but her wings of faith took flight. What was she looking for and hoping for by seeking Elisha? Whose help did she really need?

4b. Read the rest of the story in 2 Kings 4:31–37. Did the Shunammite receive what she sought? What phrases in the account clearly reveal that it was God who brought the boy back to life?

5a. God's purpose in allowing the tragedy is revealed as a great test of faith. Even Elisha's faith was put to the test, as shown by his pacing (v. 35). How did the Shunammite woman's confidence in God and in God's servant Elisha help her to soar above the situation instead of being crushed by the tragedy?

5b. As you feel comfortable, share a time when confidence in God and His love and care helped you soar above tragic circumstances. Share a time when you were utterly crushed because you forgot your wings of faith and tried to waddle through on your own.

Under His Wings

6a. Psalm 91 has much to say about the true source of strength and protection throughout the tragedies of life. Read the entire psalm aloud and jot down the different names the author gives to describe the Lord's protection (e.g., in verse 1: "the shelter of the Most High" and "the shadow of the Almighty").

Verse 2:

Verse 4:

Verse 9:

6b. Take a minute to review silently the preceding list and picture yourself in each of these places of safety. Now write a statement describing your sense of confidence inside the fortress or under the wing of your God.

7. Several verses of the psalm seem to describe life under God's wing as a life free from all suffering, harm, and struggle. As Christian people, we have seen over and over that our lives here on earth are not free from pain and trouble. These verses do not promise "the easy life," but express the absolute confidence that God helps and protects us in times of danger and suffering. At times, God will even choose to deliver us completely

from trouble or hardship. If God chooses not to remove a trial from our lives, to what sure and certain hope can we still cling (v. 15)?

Respond

So often our wings of faith are damaged by sin. They're clipped by the idea that we are or should be self-reliant. Our wings are weak because we don't take the time to feed our faith through Word and Sacraments. We even forget how to fly, simply because we doubt God's power or willingness to help us.

God's forgiveness and the reassurances of His Word heal our broken wings. We stretch them out to catch the updraft of His love. We feel the powerful strength of His protective shadow. Confidence and hope in the Lord help us rise above and get through difficult times.

Have one person read aloud Isaiah 40:25–31 as the others close their eyes and picture the images described in the text.

Close with a group prayer asking God to strengthen the wings of your faith. Include concerns expressed during today's session.

Do

Exercise your wings of faith in your journal this week by listing evidences of God's love in your everyday life. Experience and express the lift God's love gives you.

For additional lift, turn to God's Word and read Psalm 145; Jeremiah 17:7–8 and Psalm 1; Jude 20–25. Choose and write a verse from Psalm 91 to place where you will see it often.

For next week, read through Lesson 4 and fill in any responses as you wish.

Journal Page

O Lord, You are so _____
_____
_____
and I am so _____
_____
_____

Please forgive me for _____
_____
_____
_____

Help me _____
_____
_____
_____

Please bless and take care of _____
_____
_____
_____

Thanks, Lord, for _____
_____
_____
_____

Session 4

The God of Confidence

Where Are We Going?

In today's lesson, we will strive to understand the promises in Psalm 91 as they pertain to our spiritual lives and, through the power of the Spirit, grow in confidence that God is working to preserve our faith in all that He does.

Ready, Set, Go

Begin with prayer. Ask for the Holy Spirit's wisdom and power to focus your life more completely on your heavenly home.

Spend a few minutes on "**Where Am I Now?**" focusing your minds and hearts on God's goal. Then move on to "**The Search**" to gain a deeper understanding of Psalm 91's spiritual promises and the confidence we can have in our God.

"**Respond**" to God's promises with prayer and confident praise.

Finally, do the "**Do,**" recording your thoughts and experiences on the journal page and filling in the prayer page (or using it as a way to pray each day).

Where Am I Now?

Read aloud the following:
12H555E229A7110V8844E667N12

Does it make any sense? This time read it again, but change your focus. Cross out all the numbers and focus only on the letters. Write the word here _____.

Then discuss: What is God's focus and number one goal for us?

The Search

Our spiritual lives are more important to God than anything else. His number one goal is to bring us home to heaven to be with Him eternally. Let's study the spiritual promises of God in Psalm 91 so we can grow in confidence that God will accomplish His heavenly goal for our lives. (This application of the psalm is based on a lecture given by Martin Luther at Wittenberg University, circa 1515.)

Spiritual Shelter

1. Read Psalm 91:1–4. In Old Testament times, the "shelter of the Most High" (v. 1) was the temple. There people experienced the richness of God's power, presence, and protection. In what ways does your church give you *spiritual* shelter and protection? How does your church help grow your trust in God?

2a. Record and discuss the spiritual enemies that attack our faith and/or the faith of believers around the world. What "snares" do these enemies use to lure or pressure us or others away from Jesus and into the trap of unbelief or wrong beliefs?

2b. As you review your list of enemy snares, God's protection and refuge become all-important in reaching the heavenly goal. Reread Psalm 91:4. How could God's wings of Law (showing us our sin) and Gospel (showing us our Savior) or Word and Sacrament provide refuge from the enemy snares?

As we dwell under the Almighty's wings (v. 4), we become spiritually confident and secure. Read Psalm 91:5–6, 13. Luther explains the terror, arrow, pestilence, and plague as dangers to the soul. The enemies listed in verse 13 may also describe the same dangers to faith.

3. Specifically, Luther describes the "terror of night" as the fear that all unbelievers have: fear of God's Law and punishment, fear of giving up the "good things" and "pleasures" of this life in order to come to faith and live as a child of God. Why do you as a child of God no longer suffer this fear? What evidence of this fear can you see in the people of the world?

4. According to Luther, "the arrow that flies by day" could be false and misleading teachings—including false religions or improper interpretations of Scripture. What arrows are prevalent in today's society? What standard do we have to help us see the difference between these arrows and God's truth? What sinful behaviors could leave us vulnerable to these arrows?

5. With "the pestilence that stalks in the darkness," the enemy lies and attacks God and the truth of His Word. And when the lies continue to be overshadowed by the truth, the enemy resorts to the "plague that destroys"—a rage that seeks total destruction of the truth and all who believe it. This escalation can be seen clearly in Jesus' experience with the Pharisees.

Give examples of arrows, pestilence, and plague inflicted on Jesus by the Pharisees (John 11:47–53).

Then list examples of those in your own life and in today's world.

Confident Rejoicing in God's Protection

6. Remember that it is God who protects our faith and preserves us from these attacks. He is determined to bring us home to heaven one day. What spiritual truth and confident hope are also detailed in Psalm 91:7–8? What future awaits the wicked? Why can we be confident that they cannot ever triumph over a child of God or that mere humans or the devil are not able to snatch away your faith?

7. Read Psalm 91:9–12. When the Lord is our refuge, from what spiritual harms and disaster are we protected? What stones or stumbling blocks to faith will we be lifted over?

8. Finally, read Psalm 91:14–16. What comfort and confidence do these words offer in your life of spiritual struggle?

Respond

What confidence we can have that God is at work—protecting, strengthening, and shielding our

faith! All that He does in our lives works toward bringing us closer to Him and fulfilling His goal of bringing us home to heaven. As we study His Word, our faith grows, and we, too, more easily focus on our spiritual well-being and turn our eyes more frequently to our heavenly home. Focus on Jesus, the author and perfecter of your faith (Hebrews 12:2), and confidently pray:

Participants: Forgive us, Lord, when we focus on earthly problems or pleasures and forget Your heavenly goal.

Leader: By Jesus' death and resurrection, your sins are forgiven. One day, in joy, you will live in heaven.

Participants: Forgive us, Lord, when our earthly focus causes us to neglect the study of Your Word and the spreading of Your Gospel.

Leader: By Jesus' death and resurrection, your sins are forgiven. One day, in joy, you will live in heaven.

All together with hands raised: Praise and thanks to You, Lord, for shielding our faith, for growing our faith through troubles and trials, for keeping us in Your grace until we reach our heavenly home! You are a great God! Praise and honor to You!

Do

In your journal, write about times when God intervenes in your faith life. Think of those He sends to correct or encourage you, the trouble or suffering to bring you closer to Him, the faithful pastors and teachers He provides to guide you and help you learn.

Additional readings: Philippians 3:12–21; Colossians 3:1–4; Hebrews 12:1–3; and 1 Peter 1:3–7. Choose a verse from one of these readings to copy and post where you will see it often.

If you are continuing to meet for Bible study, go over the first lesson of your new session to prepare. Keep on with your journaling, Scripture reading, and prayer life to press on to the goal.

Journal Page